UPDATED EDITION

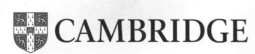

Student's Book **2A**
with eBook

American English

Susannah Reed with **Kay Bentley**
Series Editor: Lesley Koustaff

CAMBRIDGE

Contents

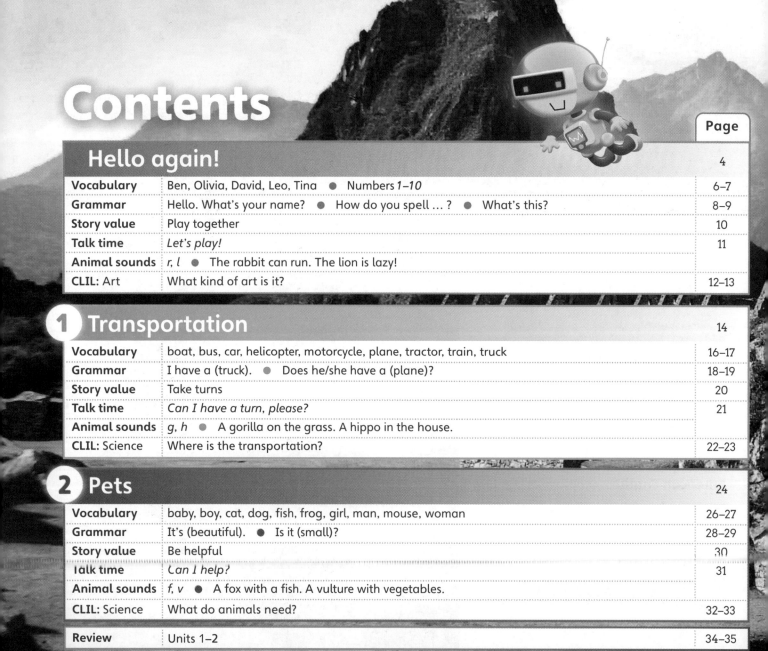

Hello again!

Look!

Guess What!

5

1 🎧 0.01 **Listen. Who's speaking?**

2 🎧 0.02 **Listen, point, and say.**

1 Ben   **2** Olivia   **3** David   **4** Tina

5 Leo

3 🎧 0.03 **Listen and find.**

find Leo

4 **Say the chant.**

This is my sister.
Her name's Olivia.
How old is she?
She's eight.

(sister)

(brother)

(friend)

(friend)

5 **Find the mistakes and say.**

Number 1. His name's Ben. He's eight.

1
Name: **David**
Age: **6**

2
Name: **Tina**
Age: **7**

3
Name: **Ben**
Age: **5**

4
Name: **Olivia**
Age: **9**

6 🎧 0.06 **Sing the song.**

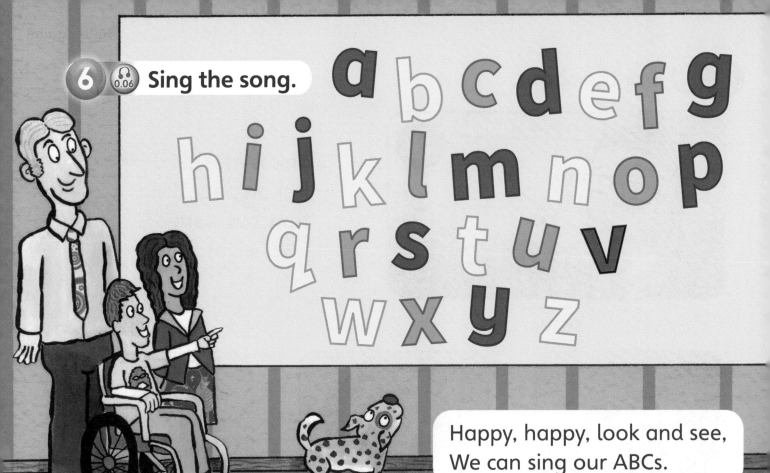

Happy, happy, look and see,
We can sing our ABCs.

7 🎧 0.07 **Listen and point.**

Dan

Jill

Sam

Sue

Tom

8 (About Me) **Ask and answer.**

What's your name?   My name's Harry.

How do you spell "Harry"?   It's H-A-R-R-Y.

8

Grammar: *Hello. What's your name?*
How do you spell … ?

→ Workbook page 6

9 🎧 0.09 **Listen, look, and say.**

1 What's this?

It's a ruler.

2 What are these?

They're books.

10 🎧 0.10 **Listen and point.**

1 **2** **3**

a

b

11 **Ask and answer.** b, 1. What's this? It's a red bike.

Grammar: *What's this?*

Grammar fun!

10   Value: Play together

→ Workbook page 8

13 **Talk Time** Listen and act.

Animal sounds

14 Listen and say.

The rabbit can run. The lion is lazy!

What kind of **art** is it?

1 🎧 0.16 Listen and say.

1
photography

2
drawing

3
sculpture

4
painting

2 CLIL ▶ Watch the video.

3 Look and say the kind of art.

Number 1. Sculpture.　　Yes.

1

2

3

4

Guess What?

Let's collaborate!

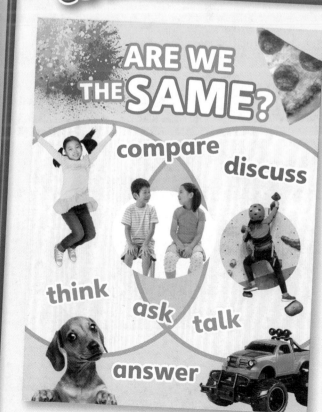

ARE WE THE SAME?

compare
discuss
think
ask
talk
answer

1 Transportation

Guess What! theme

15

1 🎧 1.01 Listen. Who's speaking?

2 🎧 1.02 Listen, point, and say.

1 plane

2 helicopter

3 bus

4 car

5 truck

6 motorcycle

7 train

8 boat

9 tractor

3 🎧 1.03 Listen and find.

Find Leo

4 Say the chant.

car

This is my car.
It's a big, red car.
This is my car,
And it goes like this.
Vroom! Vroom!

bike

train

boat

5 Match and say.

Number 1, c . It's a tractor!

1

2

3

4

a

b

c

d

6 Ask and answer.

Do you like motorcycles?   Yes, I do.

7 (1.06) **Sing the song.**

I have a ,
You have a .
He has a ,
And she has a .

Let's play together.
Let's share our toys.
Let's play together.
All the girls and boys.

I have a ,
You have a .
He has a ,
And she has a .

Let's play together ...

I have a ,
You have a .
He has a ,
And she has a .

Let's play together ...

8 (1.07) **Listen and say the name.**   She has a train.   May.

Tim

May

Alex

Lucy

Grammar fun!

18

Grammar: *I have a truck.*   → Workbook page 14

9 (1.09) **Listen, look, and say.**

Does he have a plane?

Yes, he does.

Does she have a plane?

No, she doesn't. She has a car.

10 (1.10) **Look and match. Then listen and answer.**

Number 1. Does she have a ball?   No, she doesn't.

11 **Ask and answer.**

Number 1. Does she have a ball?   No, she doesn't.

1 Ben has a helicopter!

Let's go to the park!

2 Does Ben have a robot?

No, he doesn't. It's a helicopter.

3 Can I have a turn, please?

Yes, of course!

4 Thank you. This is fun!

Be careful, iPal!

5 It's OK.

Sorry. Now let's play with my helicopter!

6 Wow! The helicopter is iPal!

13 🎧 1.13 **Talk Time** Listen and act.

Animal sounds

14 🎧 1.14 Listen and say.

A gorilla on the grass. A hippo in the house.

Where is the
transportation?

1 🎧 1.16 **Listen and say.**

1

on land

2

on water

3

in the air

2 CLIL ▶ **Watch the video.**

3 **Look and say** *on land,* *on water,* **or** *in the air.*

Number 1. On land.　　Yes.

Guess What!

Let's collaborate!

1

2

3

4

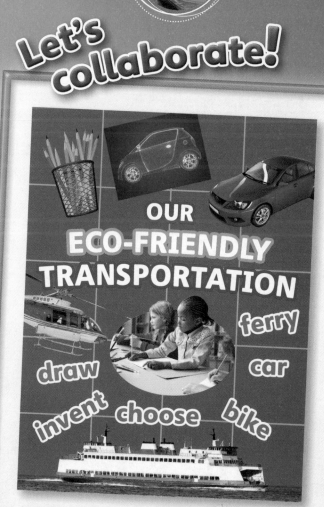

OUR
ECO-FRIENDLY
TRANSPORTATION

draw　ferry　car

invent　choose　bike

② Pets

Guess
What!

1 🎧 2.01 Listen. Who's speaking?

2 🎧 2.02 Listen, point, and say.

1 woman
2 man
3 girl
4 cat
5 mouse
6 fish
7 boy
8 dog
9 baby
10 frog

Pet Show

Find Leo

3 🎧 2.03 Listen and find.

4 **Say the chant.**

mice

fish

One frog, two frogs.
Big and small.
Come on now, let's count them all.
One, two, three.
Three green frogs.

dogs

frogs

5 **Look, find, and count.** I can see two women.

women

men

babies

children

6 **Look at your classroom. Then say.** I can see five boys.

7 🎧 2.06 **Listen, look, and say.**

1

2 ugly

3

4

old

young

beautiful

5 happy

6

sad

7 big

8 small

8 🎧 2.07 **Listen, find, and say.**   They're cats.   They're happy.

9 **Make sentences. Say *yes* or *no*.**

Number 1. It's a bird. It's ugly.

No. It's beautiful.

Grammar fun!

Grammar: *It's beautiful.*   → Workbook page 22

10 2.08 Sing the song.

I'm at the pet store.
I'm at the pet store.
Can you guess which
pet is my favorite?

Is it small? No, it isn't.
Is it big? Yes, it is.
Is it beautiful? No, it isn't.
Is it ugly? Yes, it is.
It's big and ugly.
Let me guess, let me
guess. Oh, yes!
It's a fish! It's a fish!

I'm at the pet store.
I'm at the pet store.
Can you guess which
pets are my favorites?

Are they old? No, they aren't.
Are they young? Yes, they are.
Are they sad? No, they aren't.
Are they happy? Yes, they are.
They're young and happy.
Let me guess, let me guess. Oh, yes!
They're dogs! They're dogs!

11 Think Play the game.

Is it happy?   No it isn't.

Is it a dog?   Yes, it is!

Are they beautiful?   No, they aren't.

Are they spiders?   Yes, they are!

Grammar fun!

1 Look! What's that?
It's a frog!

2 It's Aunt Sue! Hello.
Oh, dear! She's sad.

3 Can we help?
Yes, please. I can't find my cat.
MISSING

4 Mr. Tom. He's big ... and he's beautiful!
What's his name?
MISSING

5 What's that?

6 Thank you.
You're welcome!

13   **Listen and act.**

Animal sounds

14 **Listen and say.**

A fox with a fish. A vulture with vegetables.

What do
animals need?

1 🎧 2.15 **Listen and say.**

water

food

shelter

2 CLIL ▶ **Watch the video.**

3 **Look and say *water*, *food*, or *shelter*.**

Number 1. Water.   Yes!

Guess What!

Let's collaborate!

OUR PET VIDEO

find out
think
choose
film
agree
discuss

→ Workbook page 26   CLIL: Science   33

Review Units 1 and 2

1 Look and say the words. Number 1. Bus.

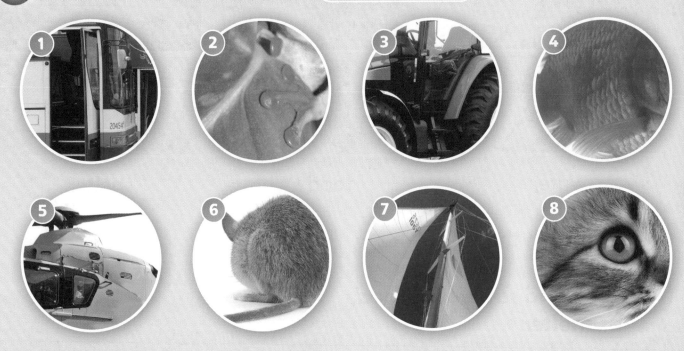

2 🎧 (2.16) Listen and say the color.

Tony   Anna   May   Bill

→ Workbook pages 28–29

3 Play the game.

What's this? / What are these?	How do you spell ... ?	What does he/she have?	Is he / Are they ... ?
1	2	3	4

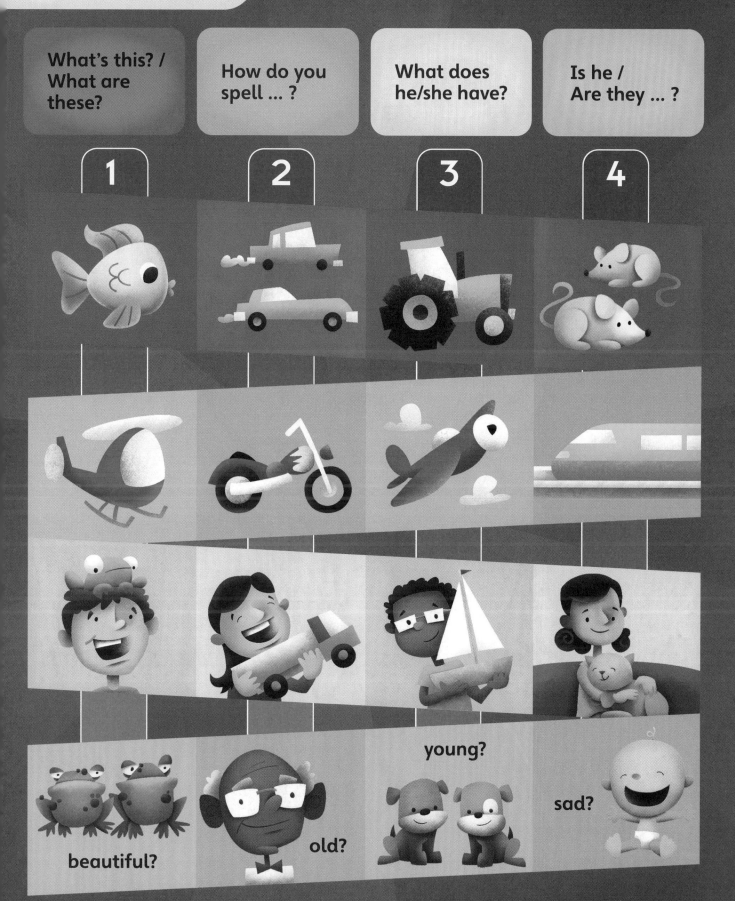

young?

sad?

beautiful?

old?

Look!

Guess What!

theme

8

THE THEATER
presents

WOOF!

1 jacket
2 pants
3 socks
4 skirt
5 shoes
6 dress
7 T-shirt
8 jeans
9 shirt

3 🎧 **3.03** **Listen and find.**

Find Leo

4 (3.04) Say the chant.

red jacket

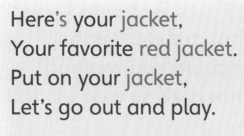

green T-shirt

 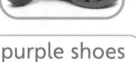

purple shoes

blue pants

Here's your jacket,
Your favorite red jacket.
Put on your jacket,
Let's go out and play.

Here are your shoes,
Your favorite purple shoes.
Put on your shoes,
Let's go out and play.

5 Think! Find the mistakes and say.

His T-shirt isn't red. It's yellow.

Her shoes aren't orange. They're red.

6 🎧 3.06 Sing the song.

What are you wearing?
What are you wearing?
What are you wearing today?

I'm wearing red
And a green .
I'm wearing a blue
And a yellow .
Oh! I look great today!

I'm wearing blue
And an orange .
I'm wearing a green
And a purple .
Oh! I look great today!

7 🎧 3.07 (Think) Listen and say the name.

Sammy

Sally

8 (About Me) Ask and answer.

What are you wearing today?

I'm wearing a blue skirt.

Grammar: *What are you wearing?*   → Workbook page 32

9 (3.08) **Listen, look, and say.**

1 | Are you wearing a blue T-shirt?

2 | Are you wearing brown shoes?

Yes, I am.

No, I'm not.

10 (3.09) **Listen and point. Then play the game.**

Pink. Pants.
Are you wearing pink pants?

No, I'm not. My turn!

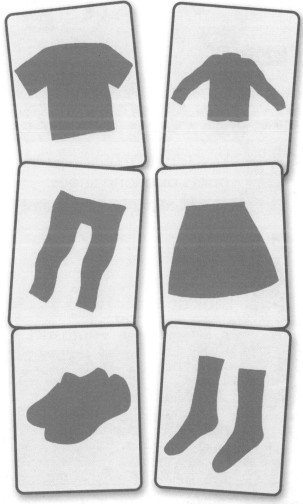

→ Workbook page 33   Grammar: *Are you wearing a blue T-shirt?*

Grammar fun!

1

Look at these clothes!

Here's a hat for you!

2

What are you wearing?

They're clothes for a party!

3

A party?

Yes, look! I'm wearing big pants and long shoes.

4

Here you are, iPal. You can use my hat.

Thank you

And my jacket.

5

Look at me!

Fantastic!

6

First prize ... The robot!

Thanks. But I'm not a robot!

42 Value: Share things

→ Workbook page 34

12 **Talk Time** Listen and act.

Animal sounds

13 Listen and say.

Jackals don't like **j**ello. **Y**aks don't like **y**ogurt.

→ Workbook page 35 Functional language: *Here you are!* Pronunciation: *j, y* **43**

What are
clothes
made of?

1 🎧 3.16 Listen and say.

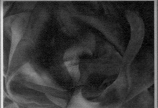
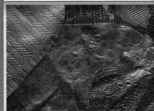

cotton   silk   leather   wool

2 CLIL ▶ Watch the video.

3 Look and say the material.

Number 1. Wool.   Yes!

Guess What!

Let's collaborate!

OUR CLOTHES COLLAGE

boots
jacket
agree
hat
create
design

→ Workbook page 36   CLIL: Science   45

4 Rooms

Guess What!

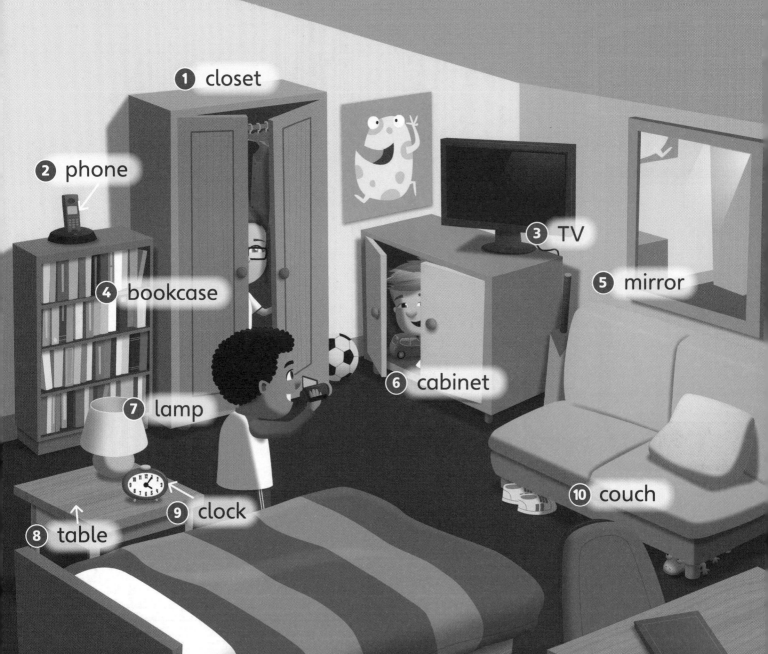
1 closet

2 phone

3 TV

4 bookcase

5 mirror

6 cabinet

7 lamp

8 table

9 clock

10 couch

Find Leo

3 (4.03) **Listen and find.**

4 **Say the chant.**

Is the lamp on the table?
Yes, it is. Yes, it is.
The lamp's on the table.

Are the books in the bookcase?
Yes, they are. Yes, they are.
The books are in the bookcase.

lamp

bookcase

clock

closet

5 **Look, ask, and answer.**

Is the phone on the bookcase?

No, it isn't. It's on the table.

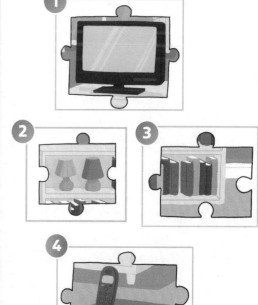

6 **What's in your bedroom? Think and say.**

My computer is on my desk.

7 (4.06) Sing the song.

It's moving day, it's moving day,
And everything's wrong
on moving day.

There's a  in the bathroom.
There's a in the hallway.
There's a in the kitchen.
And I can't find my ball today!

It's moving day …

There are four s in the yard.
There are two s on my bed.
There are three s on the couch.
And where is baby Fred?

It's moving day …

8 (4.07) Listen and say *yes* or *no*.

Grammar: *There's a couch in the bathroom.*   → Workbook page 40

9 (4.08) **Listen, look, and say.**

 **10** (4.09) **Listen, count, and answer the questions.**

How many fish are there?

Seventeen!

11 Think **Play the game.**

There are three spiders.   No!

 Grammar fun!

1. Oh, no! Where's my ring?
   Is it in the art set?

2. Look at this big bookcase!
   There's my doll. We're in my bedroom!

3. Let's go in. Walk on me!
   Thanks, iPal.

4. What a mess! Let's clean up.

5. Let's put the toys in the cabinet.
   Now it's neat.

6. What does iPal have?
   It's your ring, Tina!

52   Value: Be neat

→ Workbook page 42

13 **Talk Time** (4.12) **Listen and act.**

Animal sounds

14 (4.13) **Listen and say.**

Meerkats have mouths. Newts have noses.

Functional language: *Let's clean up!*   Pronunciation: *m, n* **53**

How **many** are there?

1 🎧 4.15 Listen and say.

1 streetlight

2 bus stop

3 mailbox

4 traffic light

2 CLIL ▶ Watch the video.

Guess What!

3 Look and say the number.

> How many streetlights are there?

> There are fourteen.

Let's collaborate!

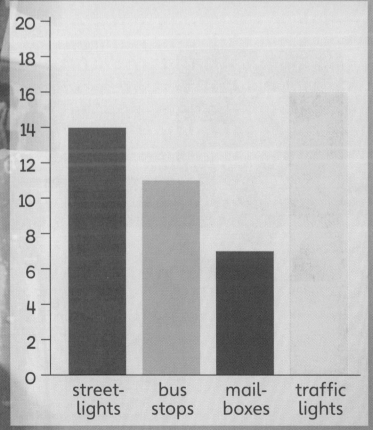

OUR BAR CHART
cafeteria
classroom
office
library
count
compare

Review Units 3 and 4

1 Look and say the words. Number 1. Jeans.

2 🎧 4.16 Listen and say the color.

3 Play the game.

Finish

Are you wearing a  ? **17**

How many are there in your house? **18**

Are you wearing a  ? **19**

GO BACK ONE! **20**

MISS A TURN! **16**

How many  are there in your bathroom? **15**

Are you wearing a  ? **14**

How many  are there in your classroom? **13**

Are you wearing a  ? **9**

How many  are there in your kitchen? **10**

Are you wearing  ? **11**

GO BACK ONE! **12**

GO FORWARD ONE! **8**

How many  are there in your living room? **7**

Are you wearing  ? **6**

How many  are there in your bedroom? **5**

Are you wearing  ? **1**

How many 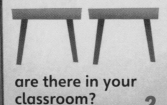 are there in your classroom? **2**

Are you wearing a  ? **3**

MISS A TURN!

Start

My sounds

lion • rabbit

gorilla • hippo

fox • vulture

jackal • yak

meerkat • newt

UPDATED EDITION

Workbook 2A

with Digital Pack

Contents

		Page
	Hello again!	4
Unit 1	Transportation	12
Unit 2	Pets	20
Review	Units 1–2	28
Unit 3	Clothes	30
Unit 4	Rooms	38
Review	Units 3–4	46
My picture dictionary		48
Cutouts		53
My puzzle		55

American English

Susan Rivers

Series Editor: Lesley Koustaff

Hello again!

1 Order the letters. Look and draw lines.

1 eLo ___Leo___   **2** dvaiD _____   **3** neB _____

4 iiaOvl _____   **5** aTin _____

2 Look at Activity 1 and put a check ✓.

1 This is Ben.	yes ☐	no ✓
2 This is David.	yes ☐	no ☐
3 This is Leo.	yes ☐	no ☐
4 This is Olivia.	yes ☐	no ☐
5 This is Tina.	yes ☐	no ☐

3  Listen and stick.

① 　 ② 　 ③

④ 　 ⑤

4 Look, read, and match.

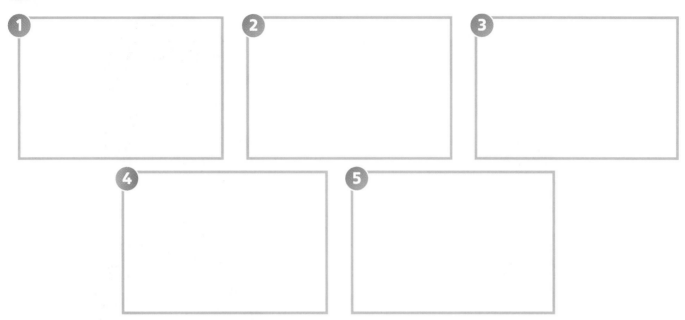

① 　 ②

This is my ←	nine.
Her →	friend.
She's	name's Sue.

This is my	eight.
He's	name's Dan.
His	brother.

My picture dictionary ➡ Go to page 48: Check the words you know and trace.

Listen and circle the name.

1

(Tom) / Don

2

Pam / Pat

3

Rick / Nick

4

Katy / Mary

6 **Draw and say. Then write and circle.**

This is my friend. His name's Alex. He's nine.

This is _____ .

His / Her name's _____ .

He's / She's _____ .

7 Look, read, and circle the answer.

What's this?

(It's a door.) / They're doors.

What are these?

It's a pencil. / They're pencils.

What's this?

It's an eraser. / They're erasers.

What are these?

They're pens. / It's a pen.

8 Think Look and write.

What are _____*these*_____ ?

_____*They're books*_____ .

What's _____ ?

It's _____ .

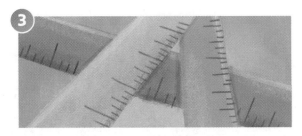

What _____ ?

_____ .

What _____ ?

_____ .

9 🎧 0.12 Read and number. Then listen and check.

a
Wow! What a big surprise!

And look, Ben! Your lion!

b
This is iPal.

Hello, Ben! Let's play.

c
Stand here. You hold iPal.

d
Oh, dear! Help!

Don't worry.

e
This is our tree house.

We have a surprise for you!

1

f
Do you like animals?

Yes, I do.

10 **What's missing? Look and draw. Then stick.**

I play with my friends.

11 **Trace the letters.**

The rabbit can run.
The lion is lazy.

12  **Listen and circle *l* or *r*.**

1  **2**  **3**  **4**

l (r)   l r   l r   l r

Value   Pronunciation: *l, r*   **9**

What kind of **art** is it?

1 **Look, read, and circle the word.**

1

photograph / (drawing)

2

photograph / painting

3

sculpture / painting

4

drawing / sculpture

2 **Look and copy the painting.**

Evaluation

1 Look and write the name.

L e o   T _ _ _   B _ _   O _ _ _ _ _   D _ _ _ _

2 What's your favorite part? Use your stickers.

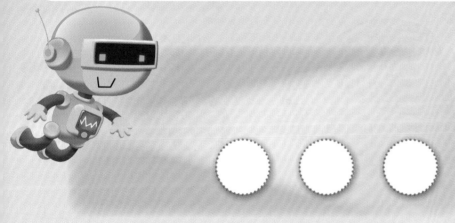

3 **Puzzle** What's different? Circle and write.
Then go to page 55 and write the letters.

____ ____ ____ ____
        13   6

Transportation

1 Look, read, and check ✓ or put an ✗.

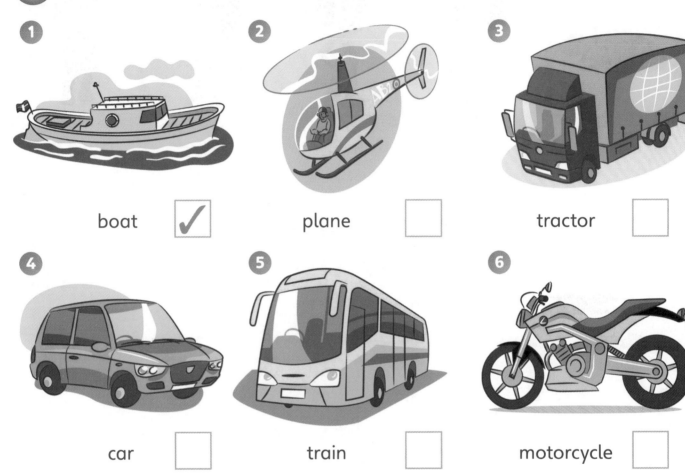

1. boat ✓

2. plane ☐

3. tractor ☐

4. car ☐

5. train ☐

6. motorcycle ☐

2 Follow the transportation words.

Start→	train	truck	ruler	chair
	desk	bus	plane	camera
	book	painting	helicopter	table
	pencil	drawing	tractor	boat

Good job!

3 🎧 1.05 **Listen and stick.**

1	**2**	**3**

4	**5**

4 Think **Look, read, and write the words.**

~~truck~~   boat   helicopter   car   motorcycle   plane   train   bus

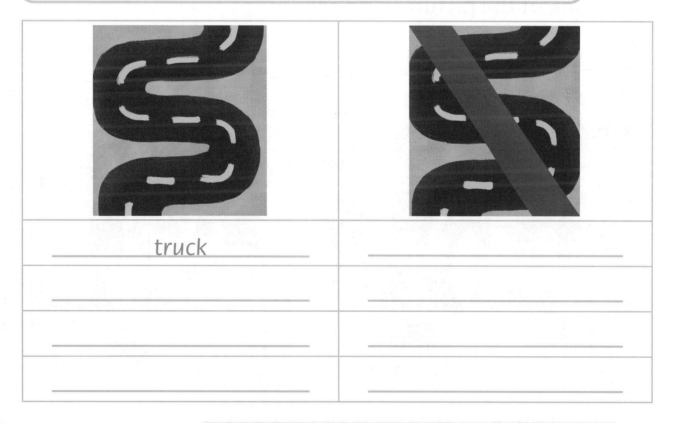

truck

_____ | _____

My picture dictionary → Go to page 49: Check the words you know and trace.

5 🎧 1.08 Listen and check ✓.

1	2	3	4
a	**a**	**a**	**a**
b ✓	**b**	**b**	**b**

6 Look at the pictures and say.

In picture a, he has a car. In picture b, he has a bus.

7 **Look, read, and circle the answer.**

1

Does she have a boat?
(Yes, she does.) / No, she doesn't.

2

Does he have a tractor?
Yes, he does. / No, he doesn't.

3

Does he have a plane?
Yes, he does. / No, he doesn't.

4

Does she have a helicopter?
Yes, she does. / No, she doesn't.

8 **Look at the picture and answer the questions.**

1 Does he have a train?
   No, he doesn't.

2 Does she have a boat?
   _____

3 Does she have a tractor?
   _____

4 Does he have a bus?
   _____

9 **Draw and say. Then circle and write.**

This is my friend.
He / She has a
_____ .

10 🎧 1.12 **Read and write the letter. Then listen and check.**

a (Yes, of course.) **b** (It's OK.) **c** (Does Ben have a robot?)

d (Wow! The helicopter is iPal!) **e** (Thank you. This is fun!)

f (Ben has a helicopter!)

Let's go to the park!

No, he doesn't. It's a helicopter.

Can I have a turn, please?

Be careful, iPal!

Sorry. Now let's play with my helicopter!

11 **What's missing? Look and draw. Then stick.**

a

b

c

I take turns. ☺

12 **Trace the letters.**

A gorilla on the grass. A hippo in the house.

13 🎧 1.15 **Listen and match the pictures with *g* or *h*.**

1   2   3   4

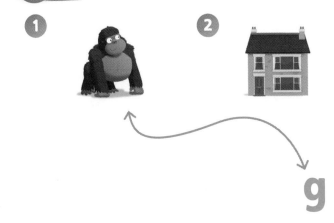

g   h

1 Look, read, and circle the words.

on land
(on water)
in the air

on land
on water
in the air

on land
on water
in the air

on land
on water
in the air

on land
on water
in the air

on land
on water
in the air

2 Look and draw. Say.

It's a helicopter. It's in the air.

Evaluation

1 (Think) **Look, match, and write the word.**

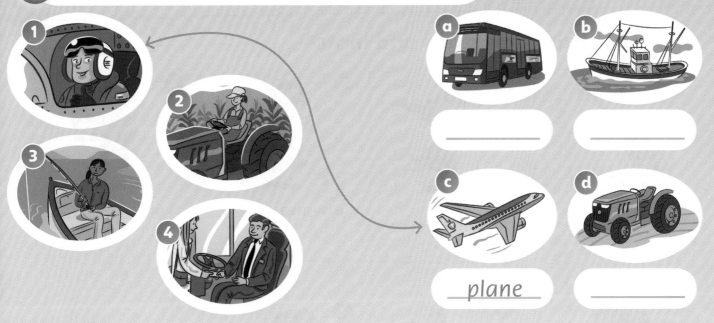

a _____

b _____

c _plane_

d _____

2 **What's your favorite part? Use your stickers.**

story   song   video

3 (Puzzle) **What's different? Circle and write. Then go to page 55 and write the letters.**

| 2 | 14 | 4 | 1 | 12 |

2 Pets

1 Think Order the letters and match.

1 nma _man_

2 lirg _____

3 mwnoa _____

4 yob _____

a soeum _____

b hifs _____

c ogd _____

d tac _cat_

2 What's next? Look and circle the word.

1 (girl) / boy

2 fish / frog

3 baby / woman

4 cat / dog

3 Listen and stick.

1	2	3

4	5

4 Write the words and find.

men

```
c h i l d r e n
n b j k l o p l
b c m e n s a o
c y m b c g h j
v t m w o m e n
m e e t y u k a
a w b a b i e s
q n e r t f n c
```

My picture dictionary ➡ Go to page 50: Check the words you know and trace.

5 **Look, write the words, and match.**

~~ugly~~   happy   old   beautiful   sad   young

1   _ugly_

a   _____

2   _____

b   _____

3   _____

c   _____

6 **Look, read, and check ✓.**

1   They're happy. ✓   They're sad. ☐

2   It's big. ☐   It's small. ☐

3   She's young. ☐   She's old. ☐

4   He's beautiful. ☐   He's ugly. ☐

7 (About Me) **Draw and say. Then write.**

This is my cat. It's small. It's beautiful.

This is my _____ . It's _____ . It's _____ .

8 🎧 2.09 **Listen and circle the answer.**

1

Yes, she is. / No, she isn't. ⟵(circled: No, she isn't.)

2

Yes, they are. / No, they aren't.

3

Yes, it is. / No, it isn't.

4

Yes, he is. / No, he isn't.

9 **Look at the picture and answer the questions.**

1 Is it beautiful? _No, it isn't._   **2** Are they happy? _____

3 Is it ugly? _____   **4** Are they old? _____

5 Are they young? _____   **6** Are they sad? _____

10 🎧 2.11 Look and write the words. Then listen and check.

cat · ~~frog~~ · beautiful · What's · you · sad

1
Look! What's that?
It's a _frog_!

2
It's Aunt Sue! Hello.
Oh, dear! She's _____.

3
Can we help?
Yes, please. I can't find my _____.

4
Mr. Tom. He's big … and he's _____!
What's his name?

5
_____ that?

6
Thank _____.
You're welcome!

11 What's missing? Look and draw. Then stick.

I am helpful.

a
b
c

12 Trace the letters.

A fox with a fish. A vulture with vegetables.

13 (2.14) Listen and check ✓ v or f.

1	v ☐	f ✓	2	v ☐	f ☐
3	v ☐	f ☐	4	v ☐	f ☐

What do **animals** need?

1 Look, read, and match.

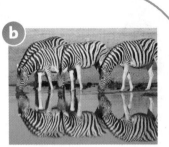

1 Animals need food.

2 Animals need water.

3 Animals need shelter.

4 Animals need sleep.

2 Look at the picture and check ✔ the box.

1	A mouse needs shelter.	
2	A mouse needs food.	
3	A mouse needs water.	

Evaluation

1 **Read and write the answer.**

1 This pet can climb trees. It likes mice and fish. ___cat___

2 This pet swims in water. It doesn't have legs. _____

3 This pet is very small. It has four short legs and a long tail. _____

4 This pet likes the water. It has long legs and can jump. _____

5 This pet has four legs and a tail. It isn't a cat. _____

2 **What's your favorite part? Use your stickers.**

story   song   video

3 **Puzzle** **What's different? Circle and write. Then go to page 55 and write the letters.**

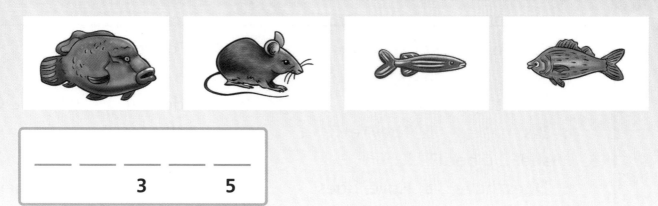

___ ___ ___ ___ ___
         3   5

Review Units 1 and 2

1 Look and write the word.

2 Read and circle the answer.

1 What are ... ? They're books.
  a this   b (these)

3 ... babies.
  a It's   b They're

5 ... she ... a boat?
  a Does, have   b Have, does

2 He ... a motorcycle.
  a has   b does

4 How do you ... "Leo"? L E O.
  a spell   b name

6 Is ... beautiful? Yes, ... is.
  a it, it   b they, they

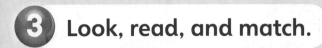

3 **Look, read, and match.**

1

How do you spell "Lucy"?

2

What are these?

3

Does she have a fish?

4

Are they old?

a No, they aren't.

b L-U-C-Y.

c No, she doesn't.

d They're boats.

4 🎧 **2.17** **Listen and check ✓.**

1

2

1 Look and match. Then read and color.

shoes   jacket   dress   T-shirt

skirt   socks   jeans   shirt   pants

1 Color the shoes black.
2 Color the pants green.
3 Color the jacket yellow.
4 Color the T-shirt purple.
5 Color the jeans blue.
6 Color the skirt orange.
7 Color the shirt red.
8 Color the socks blue.
9 Color the dress pink.

2 🎧 3.05 ▢ Listen and stick.

1

2

3

4

5

3 Think Look and write the words.

~~socks~~	jeans	T-shirt	skirt
pants	shirt	shoes	jacket

1 _____

2 _____ →

3 _____

4 _____

5 _____ →

6 _____

7 _socks_ →

8 _____

My picture dictionary → Go to page 51: Check the words you know and trace.

4 Look, read, and check ✓.

1
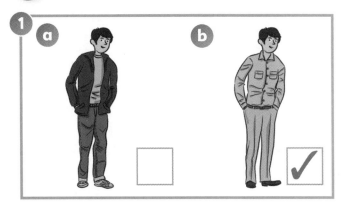

What are you wearing? I'm wearing pants and a shirt.

2
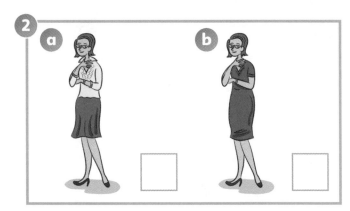

What are you wearing? I'm wearing a dress and shoes.

3
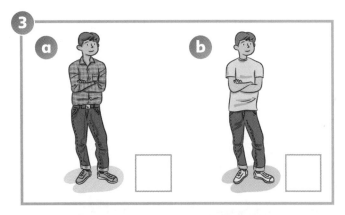

What are you wearing? I'm wearing jeans and a T-shirt.

4

What are you wearing? I'm wearing a skirt and a shirt.

5 Look at the pictures and write.

1  **2**  **3**  **4**

1 I'm wearing _____a skirt_____ , _____a T-shirt_____ , and _____shoes_____ .

2 I'm wearing _____ , _____ , and _____ .

3 I'm wearing _____ , _____ , and _____ .

4 I'm wearing _____ , _____ , and _____ .

6  **Listen and number the pictures.**

a

b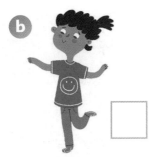

c

7 **Look, read, and circle the word.**

1

Are you wearing a (skirt) / dress?
No, I'm not.

2

Are you wearing a **shirt** / **T-shirt**?
Yes, I am.

3

Are you wearing **shoes** / **socks**?
No, I'm not.

4

Are you wearing **pants** / **jeans**?
Yes, I am.

8 (About Me) **Draw. Ask and answer with a friend.**

Are you wearing a skirt?

No, I'm not.

a

Here you are, iPal. You can use my hat.

Thank you.

And my jacket.

b

Look at these clothes!

Here's a hat for you! 1

c

Look at me!

Fantastic!

d

What are you wearing?

They're clothes for a party!

e

First prize … The robot!

Thanks. But I'm not a robot!

f

A party?

Yes, look! I'm wearing big pants and long shoes.

10  **Look, read, and stick.**

I share things.

11 **Trace the letters.**

Jackals don't like jello. Yaks don't like yogurt.

12 3.15 **Listen and circle *j* or *y*.**

1 j y

2 j y

3 j y

4 j y

Value Pronunciation: *j, y* **35**

What are **clothes** made of?

1 Look and write the number.

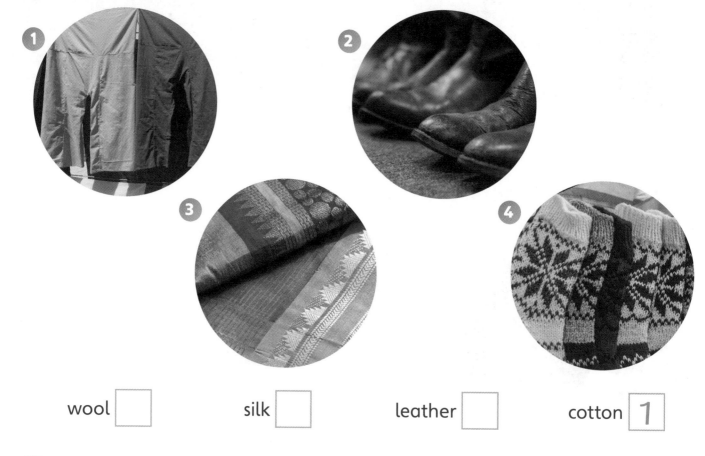

wool ☐   silk ☐   leather ☐   cotton [1]

2 Look, read, and circle the word.

wool / (silk)   leather / cotton   wool / silk   cotton / leather

Evaluation

1 Write the words and find.

1 socks
2 _____
3 _____
4 _____

5 _____

```
g s k i r t f s h o e s d
f s d r e s s d v b c m q
j e a n s n a j k o a l o
a w t q o p a n t s p l l
s o c k s m c n v b w i k
```

6 _____

2 What's your favorite part? Use your stickers.

 story song video

3 **Puzzle** What's different? Circle and write.
Then go to page 55 and write the letters.

___ ___ ___ ___ ___
  8   11

4 Rooms

1 Look, read, and circle the word.

1
closet / (bookcase)

2
lamp / mirror

3
TV / phone

4
couch / cabinet

5
clock / TV

6
bookcase / table

2 Look, read, and write.

1
It isn't a cabinet. It isn't a
bookcase. It's a ___closet___ .

2
It isn't a mirror. It isn't a lamp.
It's a _____ .

3
It isn't a table. It isn't a bed.
It's a _____ .

4
It isn't a TV. It isn't a lamp.
It's a _____ .

3 🎧 4.05 📋 **Listen and stick.**

1	2	3

4	5

4 Think **Look, match, and write the words.**

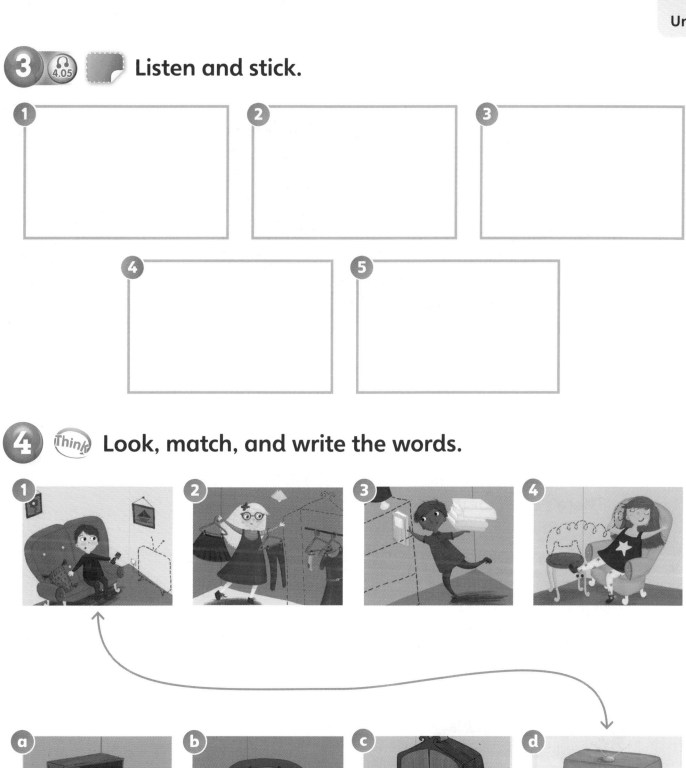

a _____

b _____

c _____

d _____ TV

 My picture dictionary → Go to page 52: Check the words you know and trace.

5 **Look, read, and write *yes* or *no*.**

1 There are four lamps in the bedroom.   _no_
2 There are two couches in the living room.   _____
3 There are two clocks in the bedroom.   _____
4 There's a closet in the living room.   _____
5 There's a bookcase in the living room.   _____
6 There's a mirror in the bedroom.   _____

6 (About Me) **Draw your room and say. Then write.**

There's a lamp in my room.

There are two tables in my room.

There's a _____ in my room.
There are _____
_____ in my room.

7 Think **What's next? Read and write.**

> fifteen   twenty   ~~eleven~~   twelve

1 one, three, five, seven, nine, ___eleven___
2 two, four, six, eight, ten, _____ , fourteen
3 three, six, nine, twelve, _____ , eighteen
4 five, ten, fifteen, _____

8 **Count and write. Then answer the questions.**

12					

1 How many socks are there?   ___There are twelve socks.___
2 How many fish are there?   _____
3 How many cars are there?   _____
4 How many shoes are there?   _____
5 How many balls are there?   _____
6 How many books are there?   _____

9 🎧 4.11 Read and write the letter. Then listen and check.

a Let's clean up. **b** Thanks, iPal! **c** It's your ring, Tina!

d Look at this big bookcase! **e** Oh, no! Where's my ring?

f Now it's neat.

1 e

Is it in the art set?

2 There's my doll. We're in my bedroom!

3 Let's go in. Walk on me!

4 What a mess!

5 Let's put the toys in the cabinet.

6 What does iPal have?

10 **Look, read, and stick.**

I'm neat.

11 **Trace the letters.**

Meerkats have mouths. Newts have noses.

12 **Listen and circle the pictures.**

m

①	②	③

n

①	②	③

How many are there?

1 Count and write the number.

1

 +  =

2

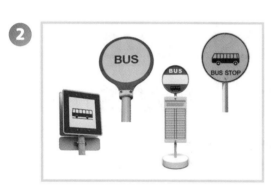 +  =

3

 +  =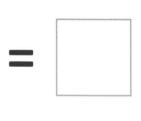

4

 +  =

Evaluation

1 Order the letters and write the word.

1 mlpa *lamp*

2 abetl _____

3 ccklo _____

4 hepno _____

5 mrrroi _____

6 houcc _____

2 What's your favorite part? Use your stickers.

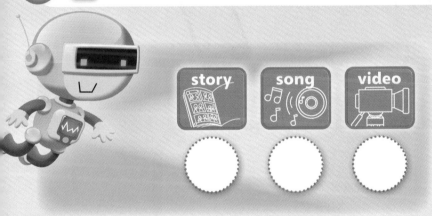

story   song   video

3 **Puzzle** What's different? Circle and write.
Then go to page 55 and write the letters.

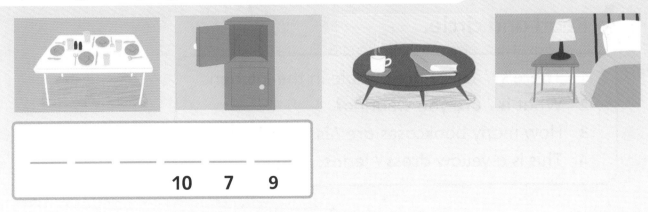

____ ____ ____
      10   7   9

Review Units 3 and 4

1 Look and write the word. Then draw Number 8.

```
            8
        1 c l o c k
      2     p
    3 t     l
      4     r   o
  5         e
    6       s
  7   a
```

8

2 Read and circle.

1 **There's** / **There are** a table in the kitchen.
2 What **is** / **are** you wearing?
3 How many bookcases **are** / **is** there?
4 This is a yellow **dress** / **jeans**.

3 Look, read, and write the answers.

1

Is it ugly? _No, it isn't._

2

Are you wearing a jacket, Simon?
_____

3

What are you wearing, Grandma?
_____

4

How many socks are there in the closet? _____

4 (4.17) Listen and check ✓.

1

2

Hello again!

1 ✓ one

2 □ two

3 □ three

4 □ four

5 □ five

6 □ six

7 □ seven

8 □ eight

9 □ nine

10 □ ten

① Transportation

bus ✓

boat ☐

car ☐

helicopter ☐

truck ☐

motorcycle ☐

plane ☐

tractor ☐

train ☐

2 Pets

✓ baby

boy

cat

dog

fish

frog

girl

man

mouse

woman

3 Clothes

dress ✓

jacket ☐

jeans ☐

shirt ☐

shoes ☐

skirt ☐

socks ☐

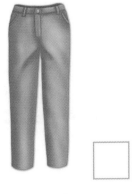

pants ☐

T-shirt ☐

4 Rooms

☑ **bookcase**

☐ clock

☐ cabinet

☐ lamp

☐ mirror

☐ phone

☐ couch

☐ table

☐ TV

☐ closet

My puzzle

1 Write the letters in the correct place.

_ _ _ _ _ _ G R _ _ _ U D _ _ _ !
1 2 3 4 5 6   7 8 9   10 11   12 13 14

Acknowledgments

Many thanks to everyone in the excellent team at Cambridge University Press & Assessment in Spain, the UK, and India.

The authors and publishers would like to thank the following contributors:

Blooberry Design: concept design, cover design, book design
Hyphen: publishing management, page make-up
Ann Thomson: art direction
Gareth Boden: commissioned photography
Jon Barlow: commissioned photography
Ian Harker: class audio recording
John Marshall Media: "Grammar fun" recordings
Robert Lee, Dib Dib Dub Studios: song and chant composition
Vince Cross: theme tune composition
James Richardson: arrangement of theme tune
Phaebus: "CLIL" video production
Kiki Foster: "Look!" video production
Bill Smith Group: "Grammar fun" and story animations
Sounds Like Mike Ltd: "Grammar Fun" video production

The authors and publishers acknowledge the following sources of copyright material and are grateful for the permissions granted. While every effort has been made, it has not always been possible to identify the sources of all the material used, or to trace all copyright holders. If any omissions are brought to our notice, we will be happy to include the appropriate acknowledgements on reprinting and in the next update to the digital edition, as applicable.

Key: U = Unit.

Student's Book

Photography

The following photos are sourced from Getty Images:
U0: Ariel Skelley/DigitalVision; enjoynz/DigitalVision Vectors; Corbis; enjoynz/DigitalVision Vectors; Sappington Todd/BLOOMimage; Burazin/The Image Bank; VISIT ROEMVANITCH; Burazin; Lane Oatey/Blue Jean Images; Lane Oatey/Blue Jean Images/blue jean images; Sappington Todd; aire images/Moment; Andrew Bret Wallis/Photodisc; Visit Roemvanitch/EyeEm; U1: Ayhan Altun/Moment; Aargentieri/iStock Getty Images Plus; szefei/iStock/Getty Images Plus; alxpin/E+; Henrik5000/E+; Spondylolithesis/E+; Klaus Vedfelt/DigitalVision; SteveDF/E+;CHUYN/DigitalVision Vectors; alxpin/E+; U2: antos777/iStock/Getty Images Plus; BarbarosKARAGULMEZ/iStock/Getty Images Plus; Aargentieri/iStock/Getty Images Plus; Lawrence Manning/Corbis; kgfoto/E+; Nophamon Yanyapong/EyeEm; Lew Robertson/Stone; Lényfotó pet photography/500px; RF Pictures/The Image Bank; Hans Surfer/Moment; Oscar Wong/Moment; Lucas Ninno/Moment; mehmettorlak/E+; dszc/E+; U3: hadynyah/E+; Emilia Drewniak/EyeEm; fotograzia/Moment; Santiago Urquijo/Moment; Sittichai Karimpard/EyeEm; Eduardo Lopez Coronado/EyeEm; Burazin/The Image Bank; Peter Dazeley/The Image Bank; Rawin Tanpin/EyeEm; Anatoliy Sadovskiy/EyeEm; mikroman6/Moment; kelly bowden/Moment; iStock/Getty Images; Eduardo1961/iStock; mikroman6/Getty images; Anatoliy Sadovskiy/EyeEm; U4: LeeYiuTung/iStock/Getty Images Plus; LianeM/iStock/Getty Images Plus; Lew Robertson/Corbis; SDI Productions/E+; pepifoto/E+; Waridsara Pitakpon/EyeEm; Russ Witherington/EyeEm; Rizki Wanggono/EyeEm.

The following photos are sourced from other libraries:
U0: VALUA VITALY; Jacek Chabraszewski; Monkey Business Images; BNP Design Studio; michaeljung; Anna Andersson Fotografi; terekhov igor; Wil Tilroe-Otte; Gena73; incamerastock/Alamy Stock Photo; Zoonar GmbH/Alamy Stock Photo; Robin Weaver/Alamy Stock Photo; REDPIXEL.PL; Yeamake; veryan dale/Alamy Stock Photo; Africa Studio/Shutterstock; Serge Vero/Shutterstock; Matej Kastelic; MaKars/Shutterstock; U1: Philip Lange/Shutterstock; Margo Harrison; John Orsbun; Margo Harrison; James Steidl; Scott Rothstein; one pony; s_oleg; Aprilphoto; Mikael Damkier; imageBROKER.com GmbH & Co. KG/ Alamy Stock Photo; Buzz Pictures/Alamy; antb/Shutterstock ; Dhoxax/Shutterstock; Bailey-Cooper Photography/Alamy Stock Photo; David Fowler; Dwight Smith; Andrey Pavlov; Elena Elisseeva; Patrick Foto; maxpro; U2: Viorel Sima; stockyimages; StockLite; Gelpi; SurangaSL/Shutterstock; Barna Tanko; g215; Tierfotoagentur/Alamy; J Reineke; skynetphoto; Galyna Andrushko; Don Fink; Vitaly Titov; shane partdridge/Alamy; Mikael Damkier/Shutterstock; paul prescott/Shutterstock; Tsekhmister/Shutterstock; Olga Bogatyrenko/Shutterstock; DenisNata/Shutterstock; MANDY GODBEHEAR/Shutterstock; Judy Kennamer/Shutterstock; Monkey Business Images/Shutterstock; Willyam Bradberry/Shutterstock; Matthew Williams-Ellis/Shutterstock; Geoffrey Lawrence/Shutterstock; DreamBig/Shutterstock; U3: Mo Peerbacus/Alamy Stock Photo; Zoonar GmbH/Alamy; artproem/Shutterstock; Irina Rogova/Shutterstock; Tim Gainey/Alamy Stock Photo; Sofiaworld/Shutterstock; smereka/Shutterstock; Randy Rimland/Shutterstock; pixbox77/Shutterstock; Tramont_ana/Shutterstock; Derya Cakirsoy/Shutterstock; trossofoto/Shutterstock; Anna Klepatckaya/Shutterstock; Picsfive/Shutterstock; karkas/Shutterstock; Gulgun Ozaktas/Shutterstock; Loskutnikov/Shutterstock; U4: donatas1205/Shutterstock; akud/Shutterstock; Image navi - QxQ images/Alamy Stock Photo; Justin Kase zsixz/Alamy; Design Pics/Alamy Stock Photo; Taina Sohlman/Shutterstock; stocker1970/Shutterstock; Teerasak/Shutterstock; Kitch Bain/Shutterstock; Marek Ariel Skelley/DigitalVision Uszynski/Alamy; PearlBucknall/Alamy Stock Photo; Africa Studio/Shutterstock; Yeamake/Shutterstock; Nolte Lourens/Shutterstock; Image Source/Alamy.

Workbook

Photography

The following photos are sourced from Getty Images:
U0: Lynne Gilbert/Moment; Ariel Skelley/DigitalVision; leminuit/iStock/Getty Images Plus; Andrey_Kuzmin/iStock/Getty Images Plus; VvoeVale/iStock/Getty Images Plus; iEverest/iStock/Getty Images Plus; U1: Atlantide Phototravel/Corbis Documentary; John White Photos/ Moment; Mint Images; RaptTV/Corbis; photobank kiev/iStock/Getty Images Plus; U2: antos777/iStock/Getty Images Plus; EMPPhotography/iStock/Getty Images Plus; Digital Vision; U3: hadynyah/E+; venemama/iStock/Getty Images Plus; Johner Images/Johner Images Royalty-Free; U4: LeeYiuTung/iStock/Getty Images Plus; jgroup/iStock/Getty Images Plus; nuwatphoto/iStock/Getty Images Plus; Nerthuz/iStock/Getty Images Plus; C Squared Studios/Photodisc; Satoponjp/iStock/Getty Images Plus; Zoonar RF/Zoonar/Getty Images Plus; PÃ©ter Gudella/Hemera/Getty Images Plus; PhotoTalk/iStock/Getty Images Plus; Antagain/iStock/Getty Images Plus; Talaj/iStock/Getty Images Plus; nojman/iStock/Getty Images Plus; catnap72/E+; Rubberball/Mike Kemp/Rubberball Productions; makok/iStock/Getty Images Plus; Jon Boyes/Photographer's Choice; adventtr/iStock/Getty Images Plus.

The following photos are sourced from other libraries:
U0: Robin Weaver/Alamy; Pep Roig/Alamy; U1: imageBROKER/Alamy; Christian Kieffer/Shutterstock; Matteo Gabrieli/Shutterstock; aragami12345s/Shutterstock; U2: SurangaSL/Shutterstock; Dieter Hawlan/Shutterstock; leungchopan/Shutterstock; Rudmer Zwerver/Shutterstock; U3: Tim Gainey/Alamy; Neil Emmerson/robertharding/Alamy; Fotos593/Shutterstock; Dmitry Rukhlenko/Shutterstock; Oakland Images/Shutterstock; Tina Manley/Alamy; Butch Martin/Alamy; U4: Justin Kase zsixz/Alamy; Nadezhda Bolotina/Shutterstock; Anan Kaewkhammul/Shutterstock; My name is boy/Shutterstock; Pablo Caridad/Shutterstock; Dima Sobko/Shutterstock; Anukool Manoton/Shutterstock; ileela/Shutterstock; kezza/Shutterstock.

Front Cover Photo by Arthur Morris/Corbis Documentary.

Illustrations

Aphik; Andy Parker; Bill Bolton; Chris Jevons (Bright Agency); Joelle Dreidemy (Bright Agency); Gareth Conway; Kirsten Collier (Bright Agency); Marcus Cutler (Sylvie Poggio); Marek Jagucki; Phil Garner (Beehive Illustration); Richard Watson (Bright Agency); Woody Fox (Bright Agency); Barbara Bakos (Bright Agency); Humberto Blanco (Sylvie Poggio Agency); Kimberley Barnes (Bright Agency); Lucy Fleming (Bright Agency); Monkey Feet.

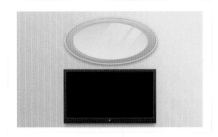
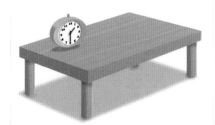
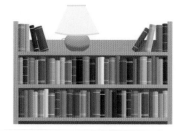